gh road

parking for

© 1987 Franklin Watts

Franklin Watts
12a Golden Square
London W1

Franklin Watts Australia
14 Mars Road
Lane Cove
N.S.W. 2066

ISBN: 0 86313 611 7

Design: Edward Kinsey
Illustrations: Tony Payne

Typesetting: Keyspools Limited
Printed in Italy
by G. Canale & C S.p.A. - Turin

Note: Many of the photographs in this book originally appeared in Behind the Scenes 'Hospital' and People 'Nurse'.

The publishers, author and photographer would like to thank the staff and patients of Selly Oak Hospital, Birmingham for their help and co-operation.

HOSPITAL

John Colerne
Photographs: Chris Fairclough

Franklin Watts
London/New York/Sydney/Toronto

K

This is a hospital in a big city. People come here when they are ill or badly hurt. The hospital has many departments.

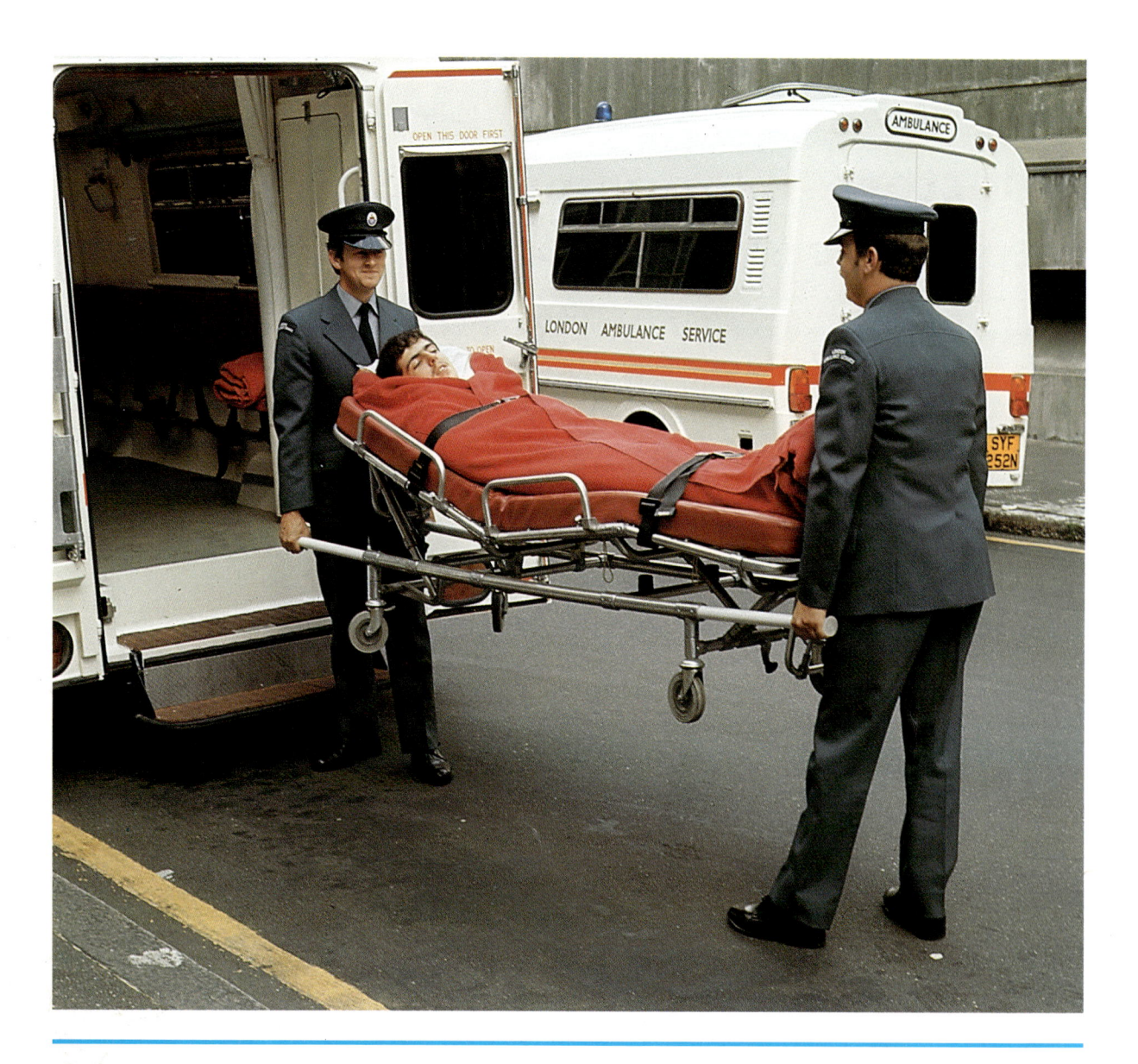

Some patients are too ill to walk. They are brought to the hospital in an ambulance.

8

This boy has hurt his knee.
A doctor is examining him.
He may be kept in hospital.

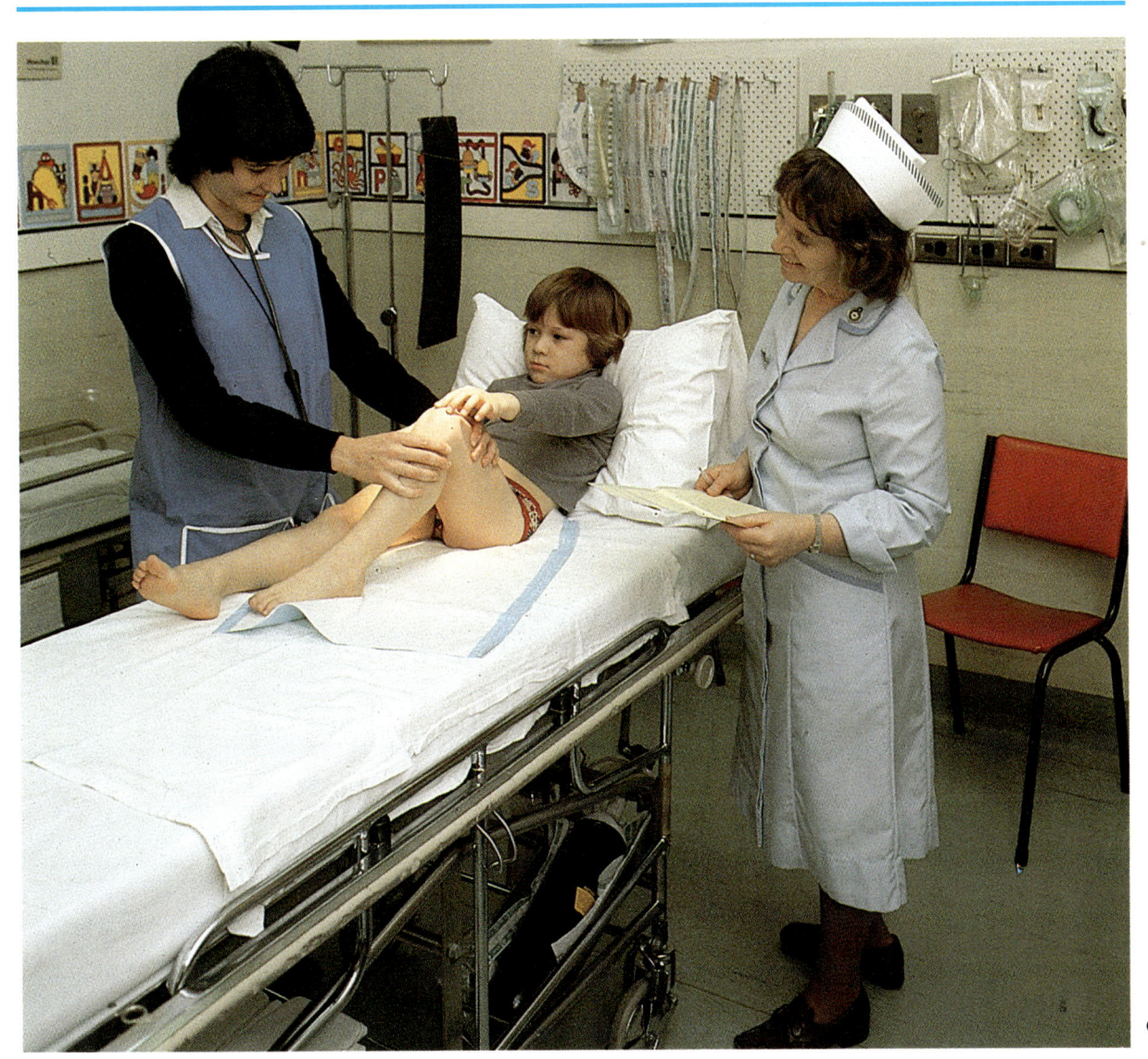

Operating theatre

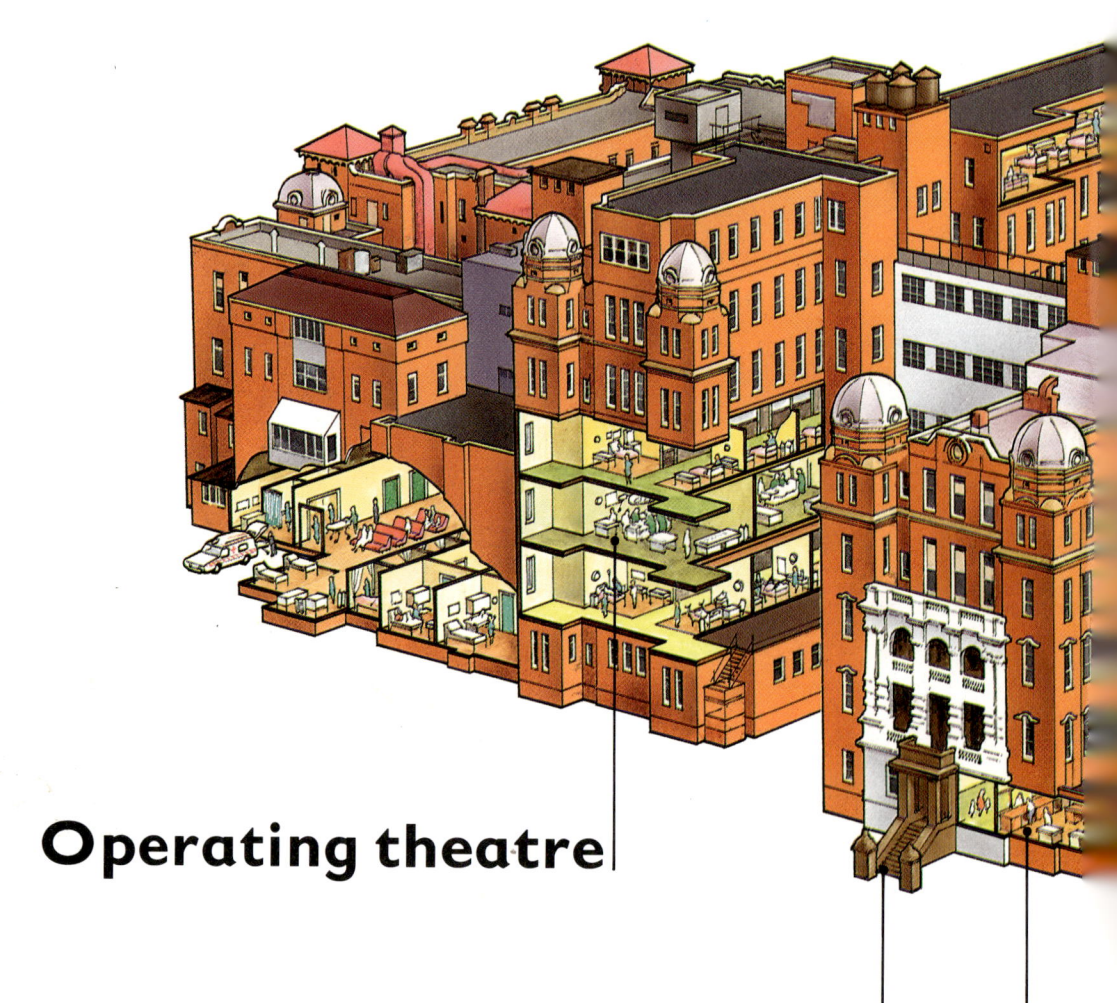

Main entrance
Enquiries

Children's Wards

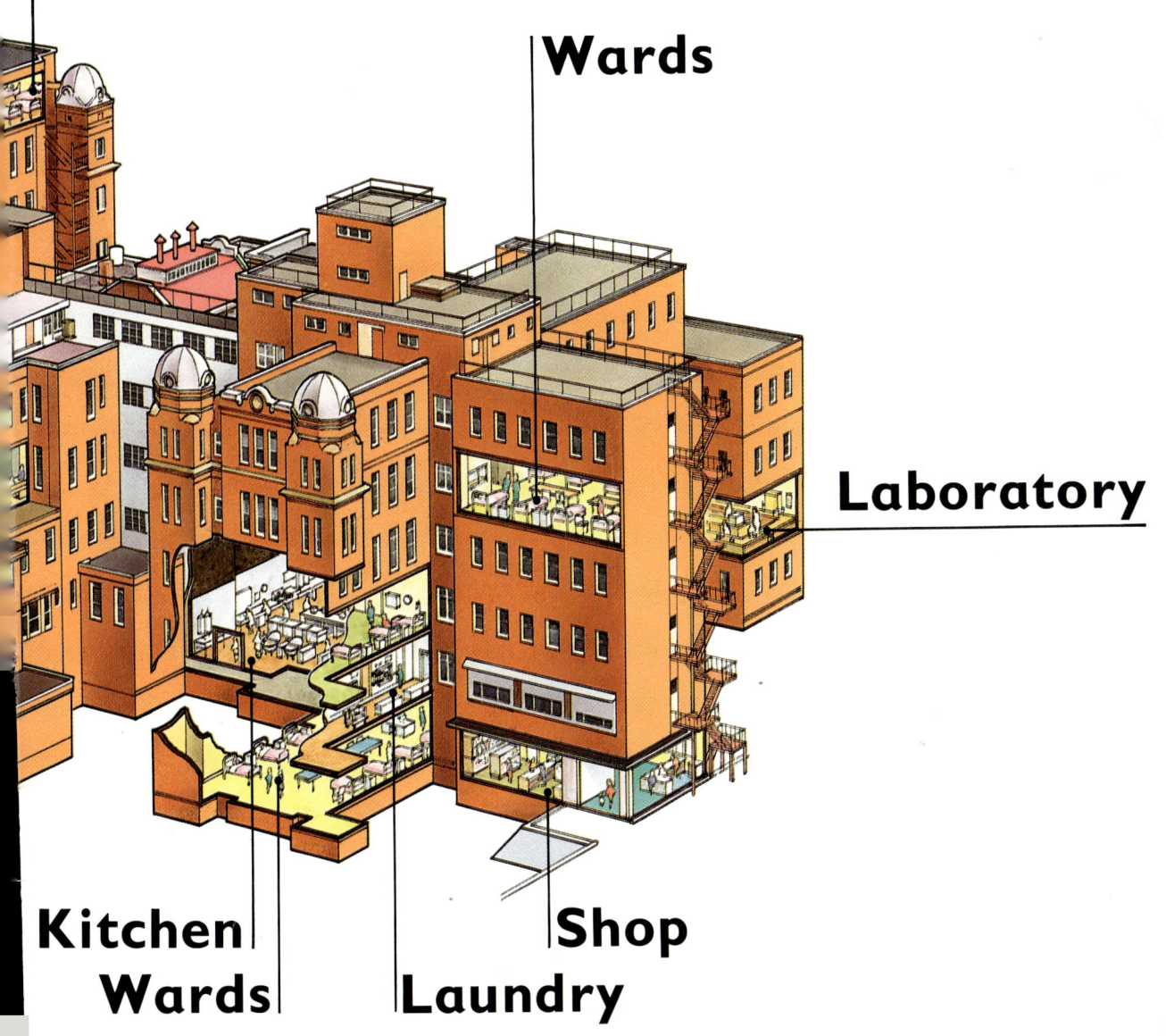

Wards

Laboratory

Kitchen
Wards **Laundry** **Shop**

Nurses look after patients
in large rooms known as wards.
This boy is too ill to get up.
He is being given a blanket bath.

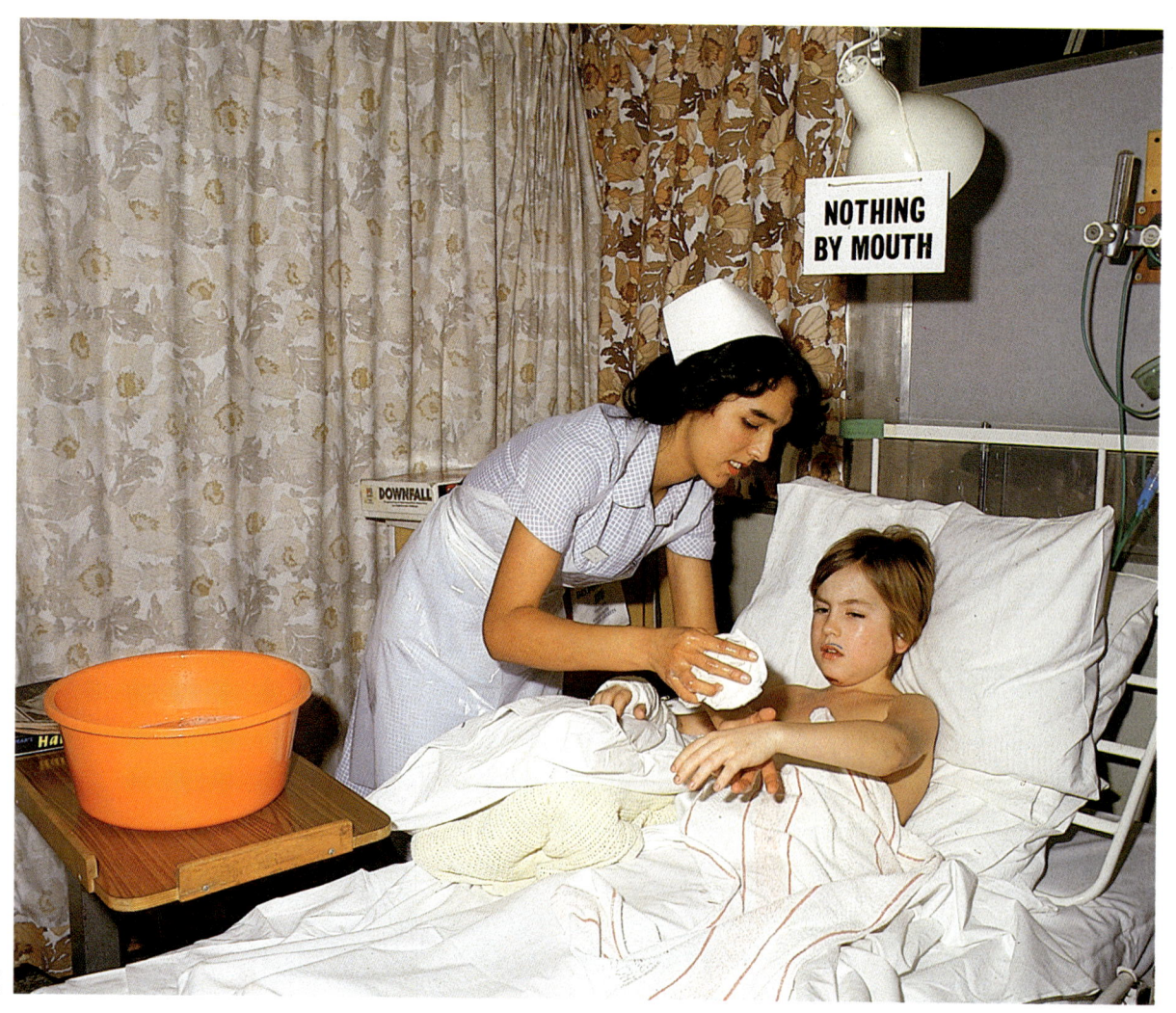

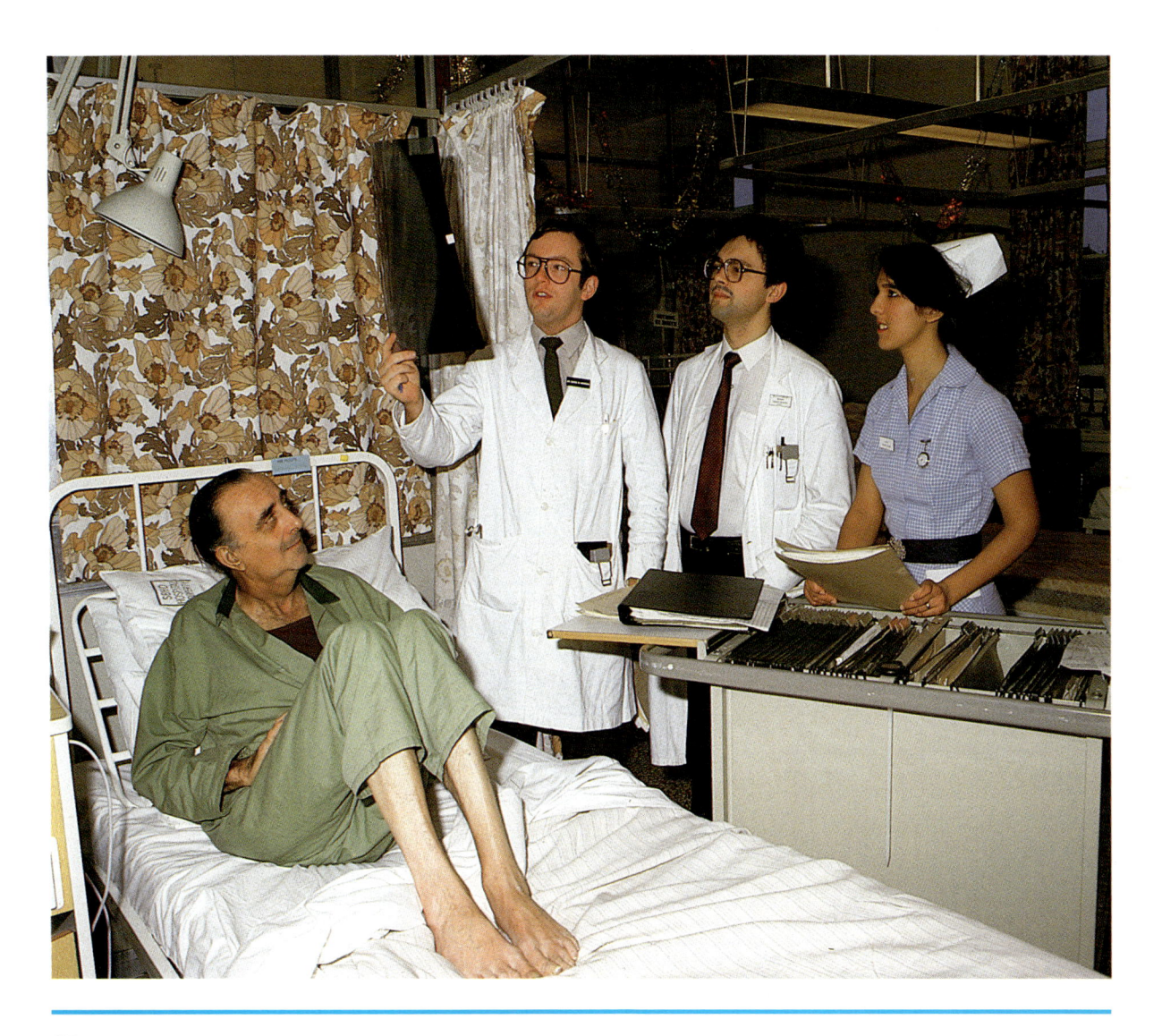

Doctors visit the wards each day.
They talk to the patients
and ask how they are feeling. The nurses
are told what treatment is needed.

This patient is going for an operation. He has had an injection to make him relax. A porter wheels him to the operating theatre.

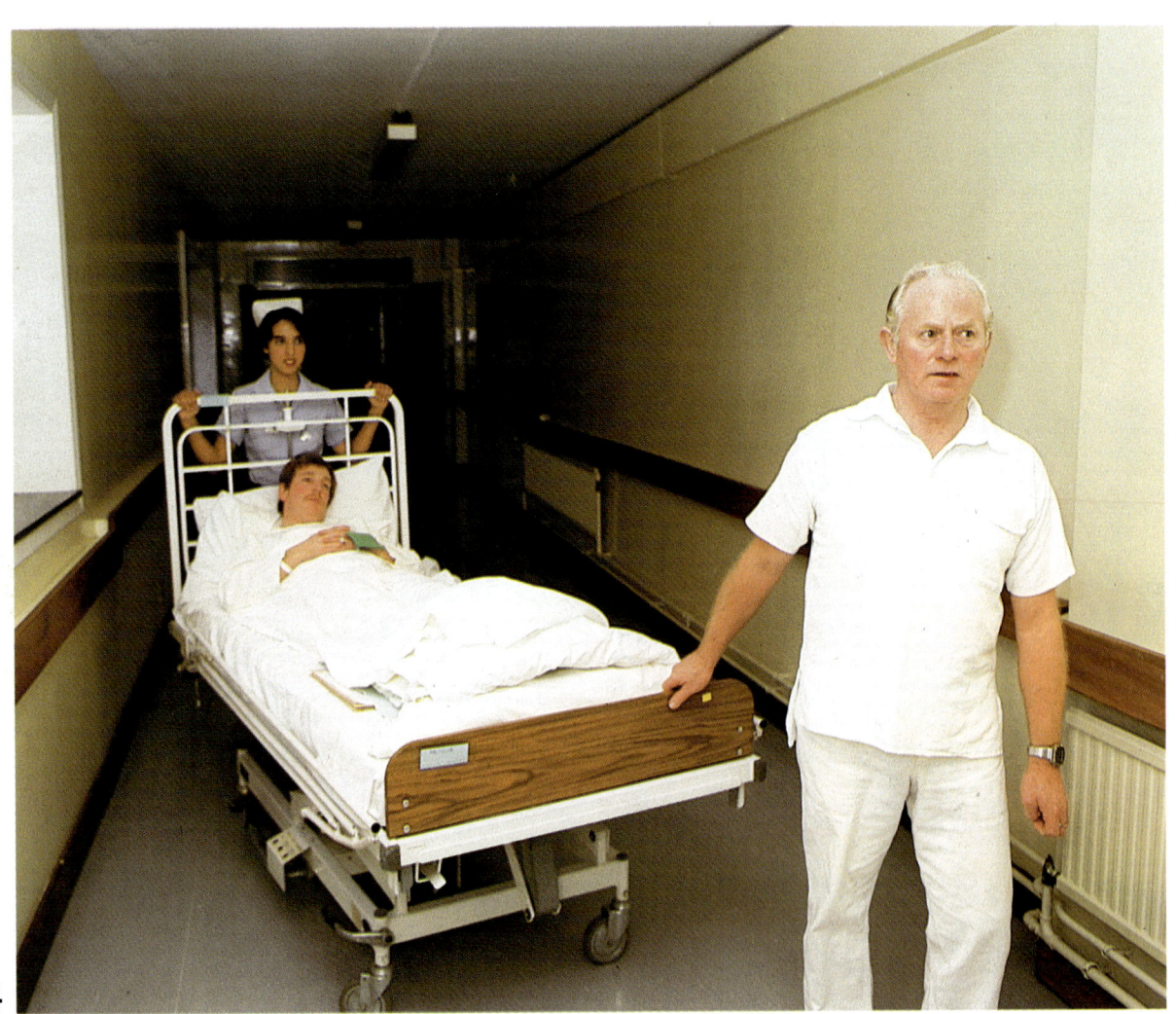

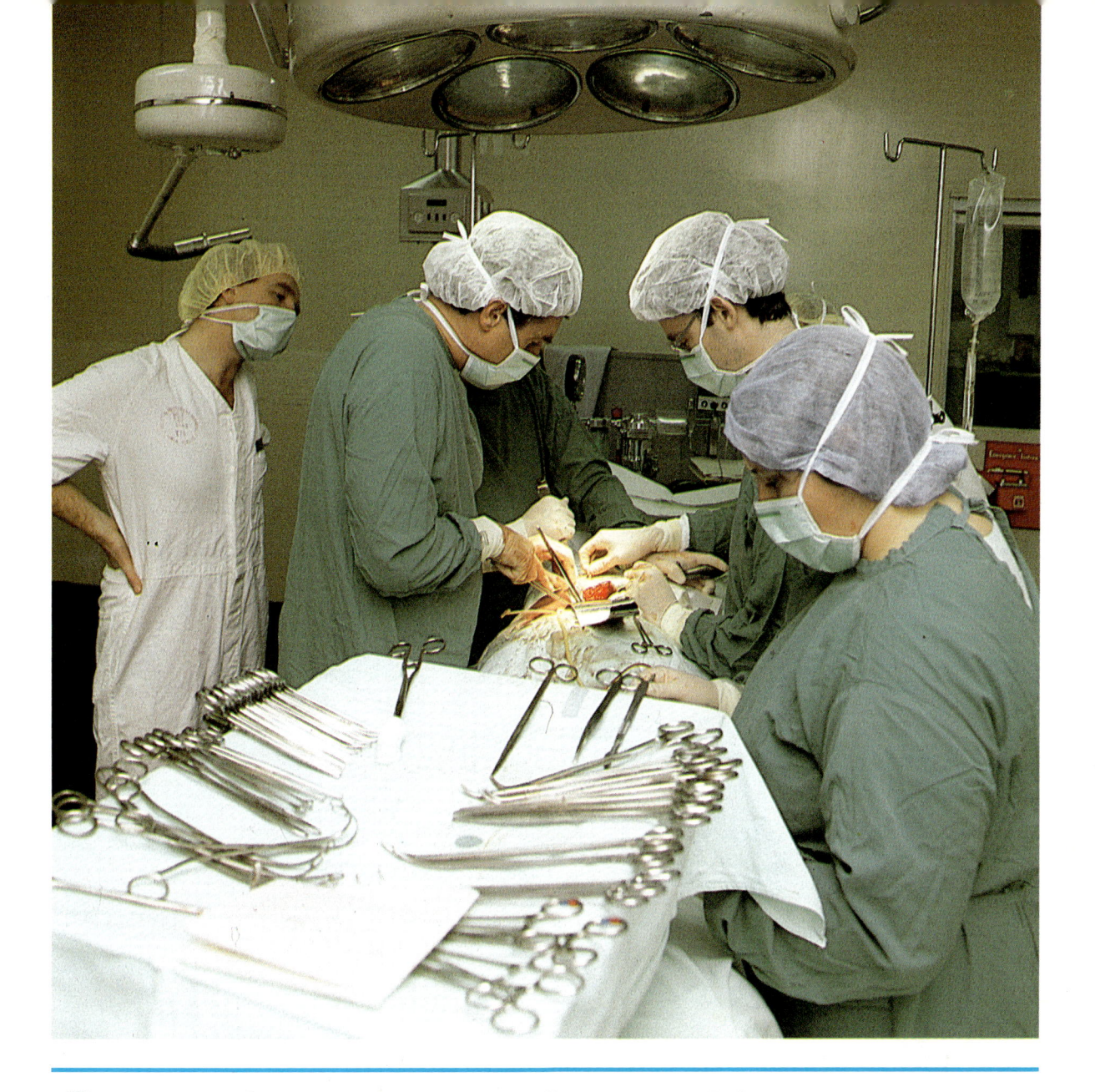

**Operations are performed by surgeons.
A nurse passes instruments
to the surgeons when they need them.**

The nurses help patients to recover after their operations. They must check each patient's blood pressure and temperature regularly.

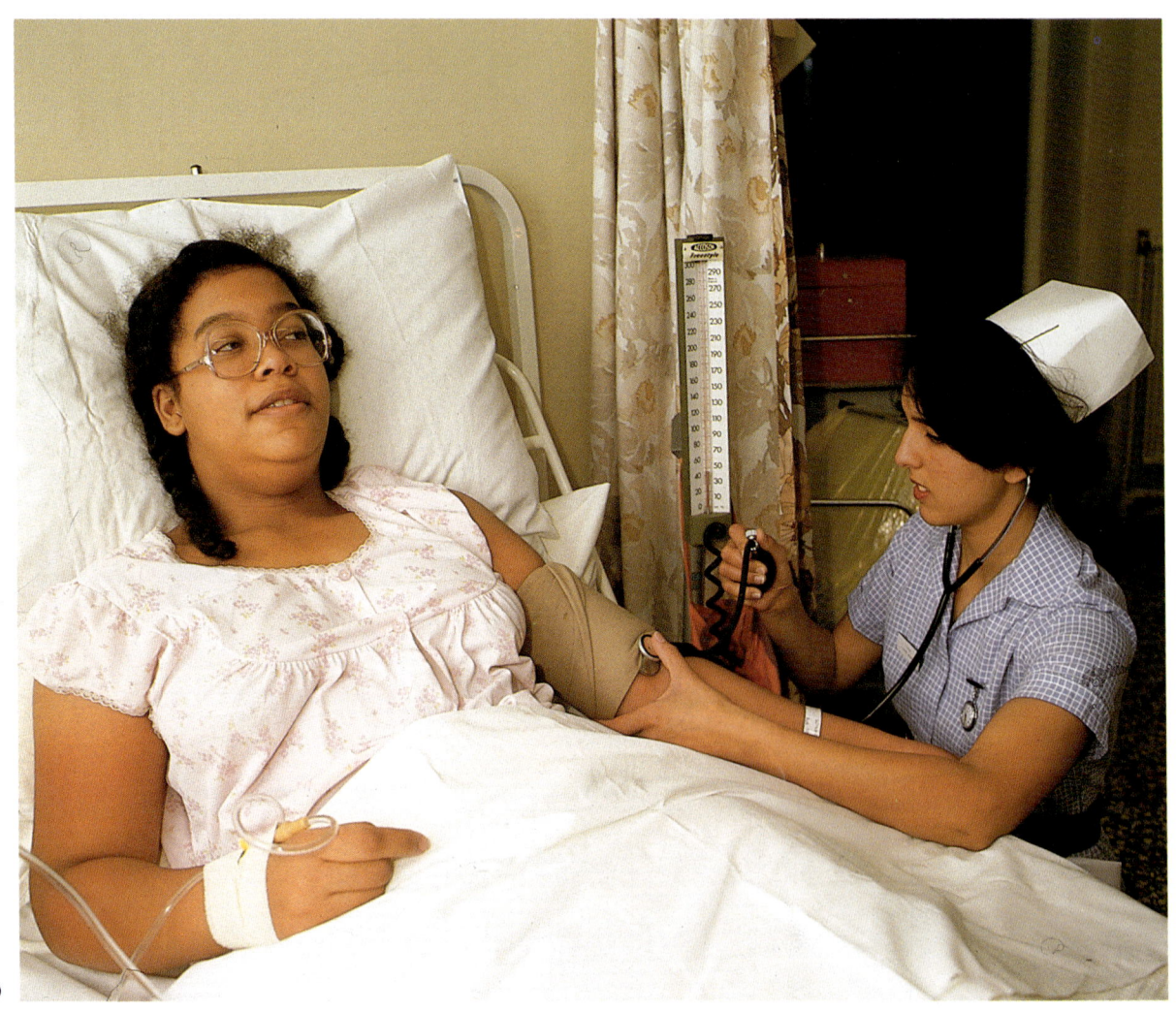

Young patients play with their parents and the nurses in a special room.

17

Scientists in the hospital laboratory find out what is wrong with the patients. They advise the doctors on the treatment that is needed.

The doctors tell the nurses how much medicine to give to the patients.

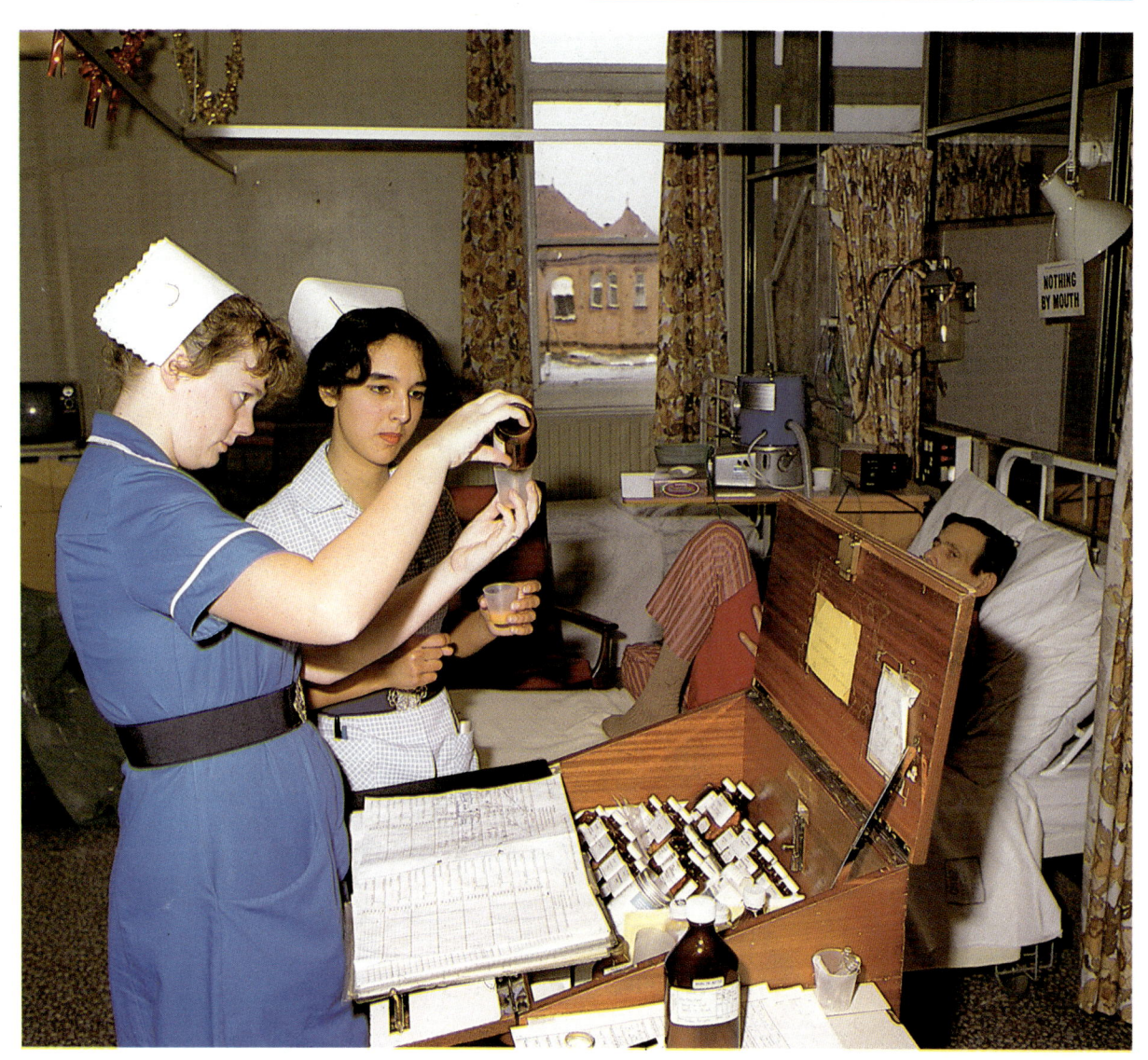

The hospital has its own laundry.
Sheets, towels and blankets
are washed and put in the store.

Nurses change the sheets each day. The beds are kept clean so that germs cannot spread.

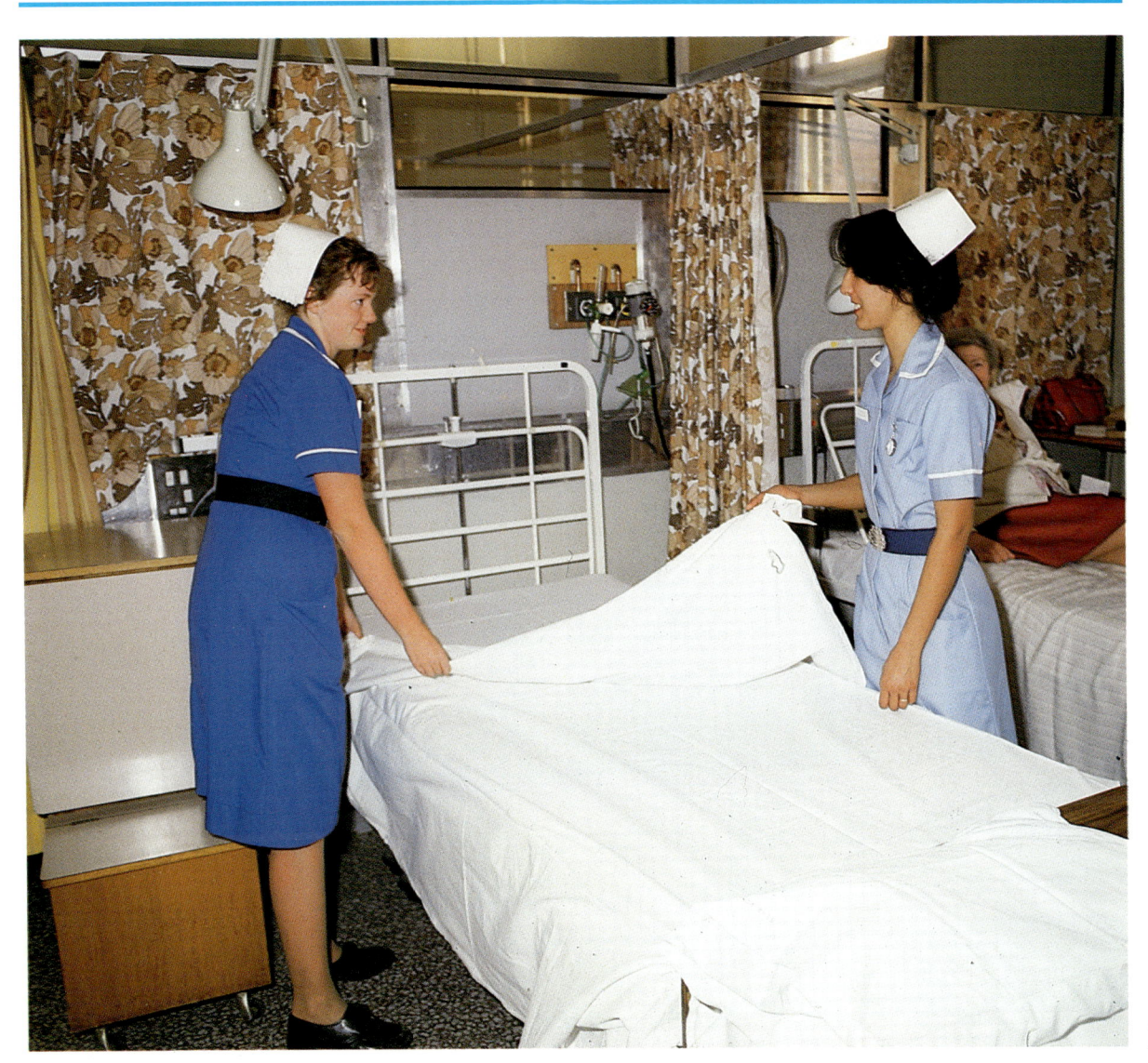

Cooks prepare food in the kitchens. The patients can choose their meals from the day's menu. Some patients need special food.

The food is taken to the wards in heated trolleys. Nurses help to serve out the food.

23

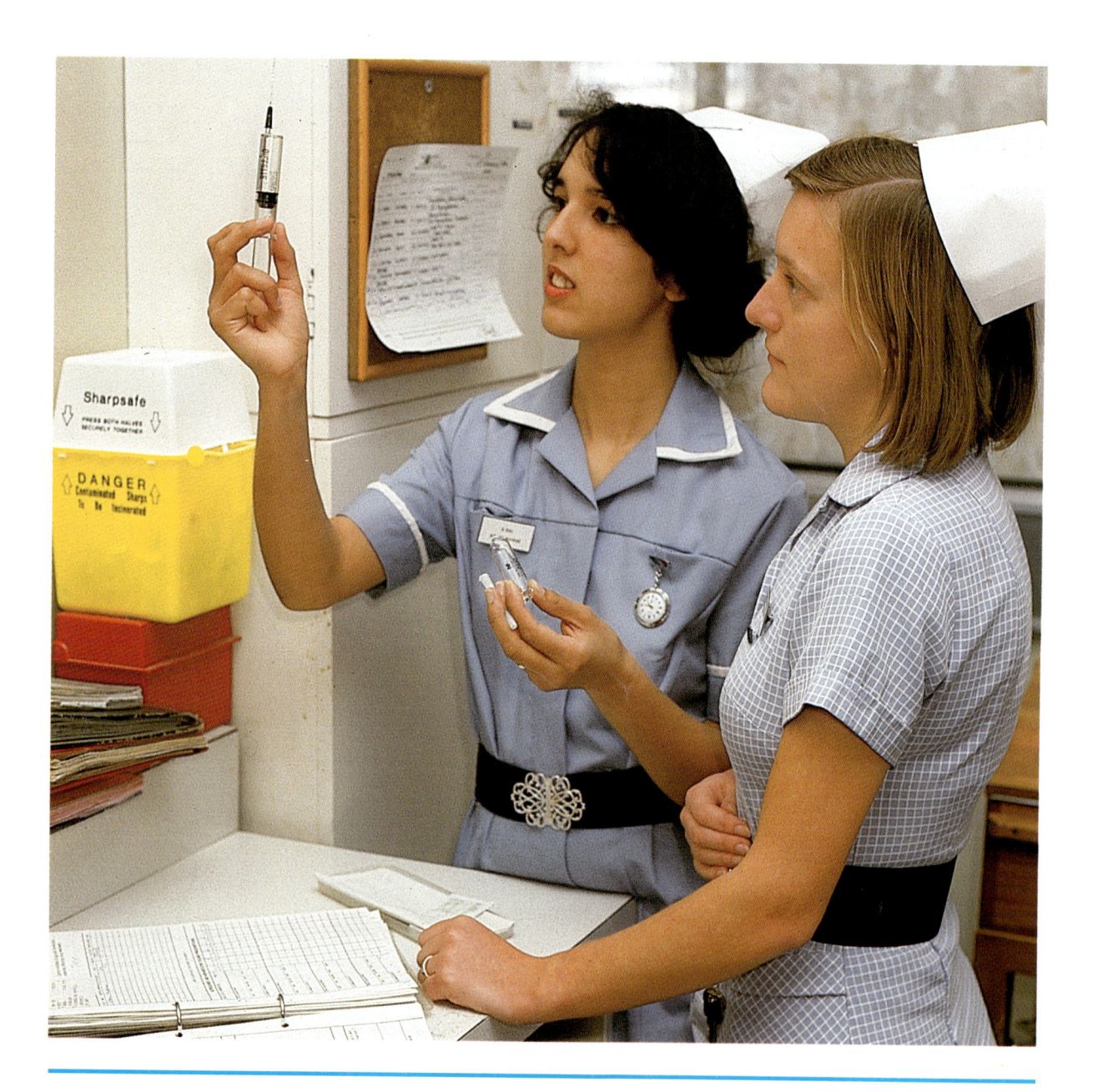

Nurses are on duty in the wards at all times, both day and night.

Parents can visit their children at any time of day. Some even stay overnight in the hospital.

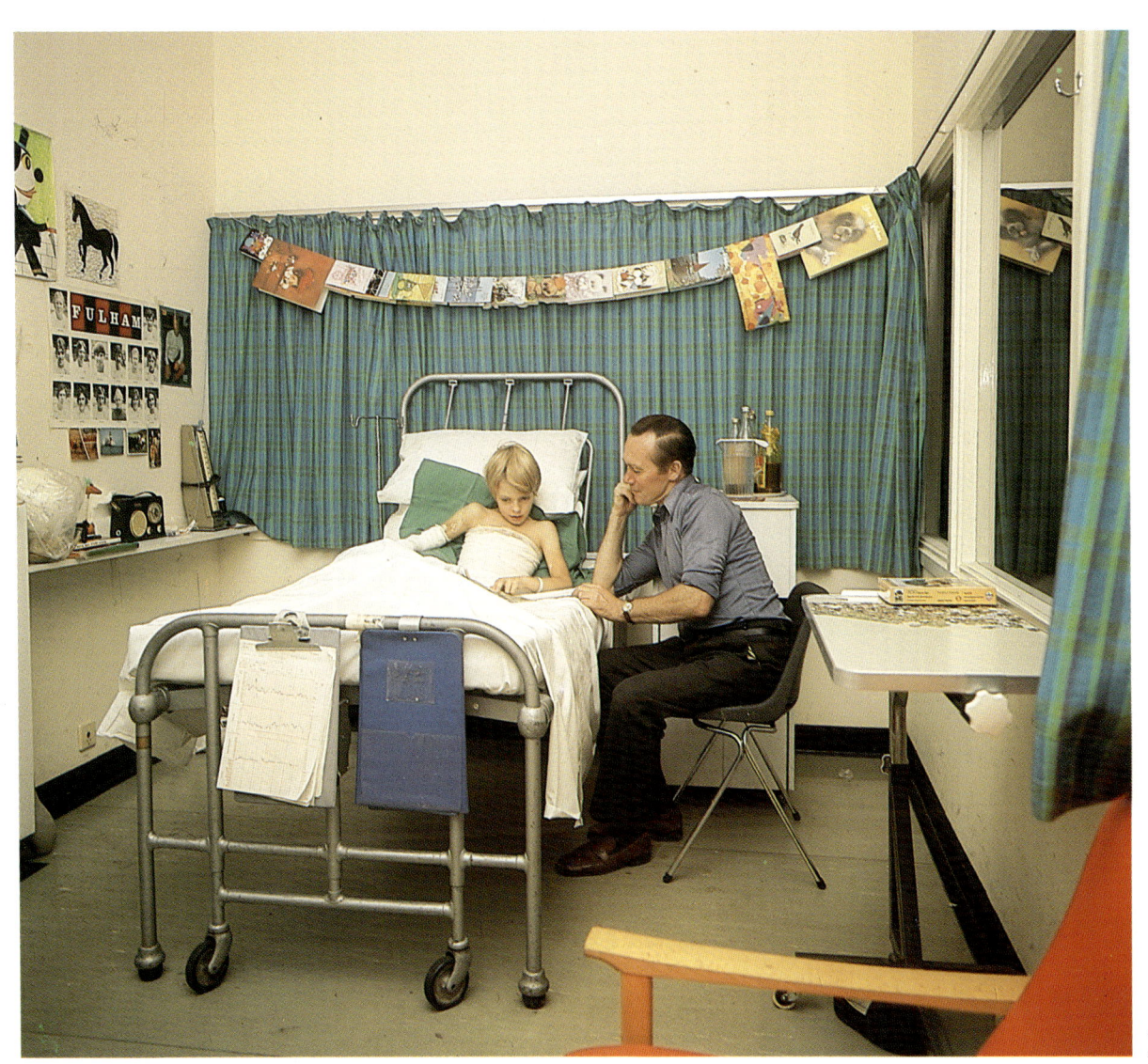

This patient is well again. He is leaving the hospital. He thanks the nurse for looking after him.

FACTS ABOUT HOSPITALS

There are about 2,500 hospitals in Britain. The largest has over 1,400 beds.

About 6,500,000 people stay in British hospitals every year. Another 49 million visit hospitals as out-patients.

The largest hospital in the world is in Chicago USA. It has beds for 5,000 patients.

British hospitals employ nearly 40,000 doctors, 400,000 nurses and 180,000 ambulance men.

An average British hospital employs 2,000 staff and cares for over 20,000 patients each year. The kitchens will serve 900,000 meals.

It takes 8 years for a doctor to be fully trained. Nurses train for at least 5 years before they are qualified.

A woman in Ohio, USA stayed in hospital for nearly 100 years! She went in at the age of 4 in 1875 and died at the age of 103 in 1975 – still a patient!

GLOSSARY

Ambulance
A vehicle which carries sick or injured people to hospital.

Germ
A tiny living thing which causes disease.

Laboratory
A room in which a scientist works.

Medicine
A drug which kills germs and so helps cure Illnesses.

Operating theatre
The room in which operations are performed.

Surgeon
A doctor who performs operations.

Temperature
A measurement of the heat of a body.

Ward
A large room where patients live in hospital.

INDEX

Ambulance 8

Blanket bath 12
Blood pressure 16

Department 7
Doctor 9

Germs 21

Injection 14
Instruments 14

Kitchens 22

Laboratory 20
Laundry 20

Medicine 5, 9, 15, 23, 24, 25, 26

Operation 15

Patient 13, 14, 16, 18, 22, 25, 26

Scientist 18
Surgeon 15

Temperature 16
Treatment 13, 18

Ward 12, 24

- Administrator →
- Admissions →
- Enquiries →
- Medical residency →
- Nursing administration →
- Post graduate medical centre →
- X-ray

No th
Limit
Staff